# Return
## of the
# Wild

First published in the United States in 2023 by
Laurence King

HB ISBN: 978-1-510-23012-5

10 9 8 7 6 5 4 3 2 1

Printed in China

Laurence King
An imprint of
Hachette Children's Group
Part of Hodder and Stoughton
Carmelite House
50 Victoria Embankment
London EC4Y 0DZ

An Hachette UK Company
www.hachette.co.uk
www.hachettechildrens.co.uk
www.laurenceking.com

GOOD WIVES
AND WARRIORS

HELEN
SCALES

# Return of the Wild

## 20 of Nature's Greatest Success Stories

# Contents

# Introduction
# Hope in Our Wild World

All around planet Earth live incredible wild wonders — from the treetops to mountaintops, in woodlands and forests, along beaches and out in open seas, in gardens and ponds, even in cities alongside busy streets and skyscrapers. Wild animals, plants and other living things are all over the place, making up what many people simply call nature. But nature is in trouble.

Sometimes it feels like there's nothing but bad news about nature and how it's tipping out of balance. Many animals and plants are rarer and harder to find than they used to be. The sky and seas are filling up with pollution. Ecosystems, the living places made of mixes of wild creatures, are being broken apart.

Even so, there is still room for hope. More people than ever are realizing how important it is to look after our living planet and all the other species we share it with. A healthy wild world keeps us humans happy and safe, while also protecting our planet's future. The good news is that a lot of nature just needs a helping hand to bounce back and thrive.

Magnificent animals that were fading away are returning to their former glory. Plants are growing back. Butterflies are flapping their wings in places people thought they might never see them again. Birds are calling where there had been silence. All around the world, thousands of people and groups are making this happen. And you too can be a part of this global movement. A good place to start is reading these twenty stories from the wild world. Along the way, we'll visit beautiful and surprising places, meet brave and hardworking people, find breathtaking and secret species, and we'll see what's possible and how we can bring nature back.

# Whales Thriving in Freezing Seas

Out in the cold waters of the Southern Ocean, far from anywhere else, there's an island that's home to lots of animals. Fur seals and elephant seals lounge on the beaches. King penguins waddle about in huge colonies. But until not so long ago, in the seas around this island called South Georgia, something huge was missing.

Up to a hundred years ago people came to South Georgia to hunt for blue whales. These are the biggest known animals on the planet. They can stretch for 100 feet from their heads to the flukes of their tails, the same as six giraffes or 20 royal pythons laid end to end. People hunted and killed them using harpoons with exploding tips, then boiled down their giant bodies for oil to burn in lamps and make into margarine, glue and lipstick. The hunting around South Georgia carried on until there were no more blue whales to be found.

Since 1986, money-making hunting for whales has been banned everywhere. Some indigenous people, such as the Iñupiat of Alaska, continue their traditional hunts. Even though blue whales are now protected, they didn't return to South Georgia for many years. Scientists searched for decades and saw only a few. Then in 2020, an international team led by UK scientists sailed around the island for three weeks and spotted 58 blue whales — more than they could ever have hoped for. Elsewhere, some other whale species are slowly recovering and the ocean is once again filling up with giants, from humpback whales in Antarctica to bowhead whales in Alaska. Whales still face problems of climate change, plastic pollution, getting tangled in fishing lines and nets, underwater noise and being hit by ships. But their recovery from overhunting shows what's possible when people leave wildlife alone.

# Rare Orchids in a Rooftop Garden

High above the streets of London, surrounded by the shining glass and steel of skyscrapers, there's a green oasis of life. At the top of an eleven-story building, in amongst the solar panels, grows a beautiful garden surveyed by Mark Patterson, an ecologist. Every month, Mark inspects the garden to see what's growing and one day he saw something he wasn't expecting.

Orchids with pointed purple flowers had sprouted up. They weren't big or flashy but small and special. Mark realized they were a species called the small-flowered tongue orchid which had only been seen once before in England. That was more than thirty years ago on the coast of Cornwall but those ones were all destroyed when the land they were growing on was dug up.

It was an amazing stroke of luck that the orchids arrived in London and made themselves at home. Tiny seeds probably blew in the wind from plants in mainland Europe, maybe from as far away as the Mediterranean. When they landed on the building's roof, there was no guarantee the orchid seeds would grow. They are very picky plants. Orchids need to find a particular type of fungus which gives them energy to start growing. By chance, the soil in the rooftop garden had the right fungus and the orchids bloomed.

As the climate continues to warm, more species like these orchids will move and find new homes. Some plants will be unwelcome and people will worry about the problems they might bring, like growing so fast they take up too much space and turn into pests. Others will be celebrated by people like Mark who make space for wildlife to thrive in all its forms, even in unlikely places.

# The Secret Rescue of the Large Blue Butterfly

Beautiful large blue butterflies disappeared from the English countryside in 1979. They became extinct because too many people wanted a perfect specimen for their butterfly collections. It was only after years of study that one keen-eyed scientist discovered a strange and magical secret that would eventually help bring the large blues back.

For their first few weeks of life, caterpillars of large blue butterflies eat the wild thyme flower heads on which the female butterflies lay their eggs. Then they fall to the ground and produce a sweet liquid that makes them smell like ant grubs — they even mimic ant noises to complete their disguise. This tricks the ants into carrying the caterpillars into their underground nests. The caterpillars feast on real ant grubs and ten months later they come out of the ground as adult butterflies. It was butterfly expert, Jeremy Thomas, who first realized there's only one species of red ant that large blue caterpillars can fool. This was the key to saving them.

Jeremy's team collected eggs from large blues in Sweden and released them in a top-secret location in England where they restored the large blue's old habitat. Now, large blues are doing well in a few places across England.

Other butterfly species are fluttering around England thanks to hardworking conservationists. Duke of Burgundy butterflies never completely vanished but became rare. To give them a helping hand, conservationists have been restoring sunny glades in woodlands where primroses and cowslips bloom. This means their caterpillars have the right habitat and the right plants to eat. Therefore, Duke of Burgundies are slowly coming back.

# Searching for the Harlequin Toad's Superpower

Overlooking the Caribbean coast in the north of Colombia is a towering mountain range covered in forests and home to howler monkeys, peccaries, jaguars and tapirs. Also living on the Sierra Nevada de Santa Marta are many species of amphibians, including glass frogs and rain frogs, that live here and nowhere else. There are at least four species of harlequin toads — among the most endangered group of amphibians in the world. But on this Colombian mountain, the harlequins are hopping about in good numbers. But how are they surviving?

In the 1980s, a terrible amphibian disease began to sweep around the world. The deadly fungus, known as chytrid, infects the skin of frogs, toads and salamanders, stopping them from getting the salts they need to survive. Eventually their hearts stop beating. Chytrid has caused many amphibian populations to collapse and species to go extinct — including many harlequin toads. That's why scientists were amazed to find healthy harlequins living on Sierra Nevada de Santa Marta. One of them, the starry night harlequin, hadn't been seen by scientists for 30 years. These toads are sacred to the region's indigenous Arhuaco community who live on the mountain. In 2019, members of the community gave scientists permission to visit and photograph the toads.

Scientists are working hard to figure out what's protecting Colombia's harlequins from deadly chytrid infections. Along with the conservation efforts of the indigenous Arhuaco community, they may have developed their own defenses against the fungus. Whatever it is, harlequins could hold the key to saving other endangered amphibians around the world.

# A Flourishing Coral Reef Home

Imagine being as free as a fish! There are no hard boundaries or fences in the ocean to stop fish and other animals from swimming off but these marine creatures often cannot escape the threat of overfishing by big, industrial fishing boats. However, conservationists have found that protecting parts of the ocean from fishing can help revive whole ecosystems. Marine reserves are places where no fishing is allowed and they can work brilliantly, even quite small ones.

Some decades ago, the coral reef at Cabo Pulmo in Mexico's Gulf of California was suffering badly from overfishing. People in the local fishing community decided to help the coral reef recover and asked the Mexican government for help. Together they set up the Cabo Pulmo National Marine Park. Right off the tiny village called Cabo Pulmo, this national marine park has become a world-famous success story for ocean protection.

Cabo Pulmo is home to masses of species. There are sharks and rays, parrotfish, triggerfish, snappers and boxfish. The reef has also become a shelter for gulf groupers. These big fish used to be rare in the area but now they live longer and have more babies in the safety of Cabo Pulmo.

Diving marine biologists have been counting fishes at Cabo Pulmo and working out their total weight — called the biomass. After just 14 years, fish biomass inside the reserve had increased by 463 percent. No one had ever seen such an amazing recovery of fish in a marine reserve and the success of Cabo Pulmo comes down to the local community who protect the reef.

# Extreme Science Saving Āhinahina

Near the peak of Mauna Kea, the highest volcano in Hawai'i, scientists have gone to extreme lengths to save a species. The plant specialists, called botanists, dangled from climbing ropes and lowered themselves down steep cliffs and into narrow gorges. They searched for rare, silvery plants that can live for over 90 years and flower just once before they die.

Āhinahina, also known as silverswords, used to grow all over Mauna Kea. Their covering of silvery hairs helps them to reflect the bright sun and survive in the dry, ashy desert of the tall volcano. But more than 200 years ago, European travelers introduced goats and sheep which ate most of these special plants. By the 1990s, the only silverswords left were tucked away in inaccessible places.

The climbing botanists searched for flowers and carefully gathered yellow pollen grains. Using a paintbrush, they transferred the pollen to other flowers which were often a long distance away. They were doing what the missing bees and moths would have done. Later, the botanists collected the resulting seeds and grew them in greenhouses, before they replanted the seedlings out on the mountain. Compared to a few decades ago, there are now many more silverswords in the wild. To add to the silverswords' troubles, introduced species of ants and wasps threaten the bees and moths that are their native pollinators. Without them, silverswords need a helping hand.

# Return of the Turtles

During the coronavirus pandemic, when so many people stayed home, wild animals had a lot more peaceful space to themselves. On Phuket Island in Thailand, beaches that were normally busy with tourists fell quiet. Hotels closed and switched off their lights. And during these dark nights, rare visitors arrived.

11 huge female leatherback sea turtles crawled across the sand to lay their eggs. That year, 351 turtle hatchlings climbed out of their nests and scrambled across the beach to the sea, led by moonlight glinting on the waves. This was the largest number of nesting sea turtles that the island had seen in 20 years. There's no doubt that bright hotel lights puzzle hatchlings and draw them inland. Nesting female turtles need quiet and dark places to lay their eggs. While the pandemic has been linked to an increase in sea turtle nesting, both in Thailand and elsewhere in the world, scientists are worried that we will soon be back to square one if we don't control tourism.

The good news is there are signs some turtle species are recovering after 60 years of conservation measures. Scuba divers counting turtles around islands in the Pacific have seen the number of green turtles going up. Turtles used to be killed for their meat, shells and eggs, but now laws around the world protect them. Many fisheries used to accidentally catch and drown turtles but now use nets fitted with escape hatches so the turtles can swim free.

If more turtle populations are to recover, they need continuing conservation care. This will mean they need looking after on the nesting beaches that are threatened by rising sea levels, and monitoring all throughout their long adult lives as they roam the open ocean.

# Watching the Tigers Return

A century ago, 100,000 tigers roamed the wild. By 2010, there were only around 3,000 left. That year a new plan began, to double the number of tigers by 2022 — the Chinese Year of the Tiger. In one country in particular, tigers seem to be doing much better than they were.

In India, shooting tigers was a popular sport in the time of the British Empire. The British Crown held hunting parties as a royal sport and killed tens of thousands of tigers. Now it's illegal to shoot tigers, but for poachers in India it's worth the risk of going to prison because they can make a lot of money selling tiger parts. Medicinal potions are made from tiger bones, teeth, whiskers, claws and blood, even though there's no scientific proof they work.

However, there are also lots of people working hard to protect India's tigers and their forest homes. Over 50 tiger reserves have been set up, including Ranthambore in northwest India. Part of the money tourists pay to visit them goes to people who live nearby meaning local communities are invested in protecting these beautiful creatures.

Every four years there's a tiger count. People set out camera traps and search for tiger footprints and scat, or poo. In 2018, when the last survey took place, the numbers looked promising, with almost 3,000 tigers counted in India alone. But tigers are hard to spot and some scientists think the surveys are not very accurate. Even so, most agree that tigers are thriving in reserves in central India. The future for tigers depends on many things. More tiger habitat needs protecting and the trade in all tiger products must end. But the success of reserves like Ranthambore show the positive results that are possible.

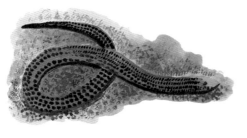

# Finding a Lost Chameleon

Many species around the world have been 'lost', often meaning they just haven't been seen for a long time. Some could still be out there in the wild but scientists haven't been in the right place at the right time to spot them and prove they haven't gone extinct. A team went to look for one of those species in the last place it was seen a century ago on the Indian Ocean island of Madagascar. They searched through long, rainy nights but didn't find what they were looking for. Then one day they got lucky.

Chameleons can be hard to spot, especially in the dry forests of northwest Madagascar. Eggs hatch when the short rainy season begins each year. Young chameleons quickly grow and lay their own eggs, then after four or five months they die. To find these hidden reptiles, biologists must work through the rainy season, when roads flood and many places get cut off.

The last confirmed sighting of Voeltzkow's chameleon – named after a German zoologist called Alfred who collected the species – was back in 1913. In 2018, chameleon hunters braved the downpours and scoured forests. Eventually they found the chameleons in an overgrown hotel garden. Madame Chabaud, the hotel's owner, said she usually saw lots of the colorful chameleons when the rains came each year.

Other supposed 'lost' species in Madagascar include a blind snake, a skink and a tiny Brookesia chameleon that would sit on your fingertip, and will no doubt be even harder to find! The rediscovery of Voeltzkow's chameleon gives us hope about the possibility of finding other 'lost' and never-before-seen species in the future.

# Replanting Seagrass Meadows

Vast green meadows of eelgrass used to grow in the sheltered, saltwater lagoons of Virginia on the US east coast. But in the 1930s, a deadly slime mold began killing the underwater grasses. And when a devastating hurricane hit, the stressed ecosystem completely collapsed. For decades there were no seagrasses to be seen until scuba diving scientists spotted a few patches holding on, which gave them an idea. Maybe they could replant the lost meadows.

Eelgrass is one of many species of seagrasses which grow in shallow seas worldwide. They look like seaweed but in fact they're flowering plants, just like grasses on land. Their tiny flowers and seeds are the secrets to their successful return.

Starting in 1999, divers collected seeds from other healthy seagrass meadows and scattered them across the bays of Virginia. The seeds sprouted and the green ecosystems began to return. Since then, divers have spread more than 70 million seeds and over 15,500 acres of new seagrass meadow has grown. Other lost species have also come back to the bays of Virginia. Scallops, pinfish, silversides and blue crabs have all naturally returned, and tundra swans, redhead ducks and other visiting birds have also increased. The ecosystem is thriving.

Seagrass rewilding projects are now underway elsewhere too, including in Wales and New Zealand. Seagrasses can soak up carbon 35 times faster than rainforests. So, the more seagrass meadows there are, the better.

# Protecting Burrowing Parrots

On the lower slopes of the Andean Mountains in central Chile, the Río de los Cipreses National Reserve has saved burrowing parrots from the edge of extinction. Over 35 years ago, there were only a few hundred of these birds alive. Now there are thousands.

Not long ago, parrot traffickers would climb down steep ravines on ropes and use long hooks to reach into the burrows and steal chicks from their nests. The parrots' colorful plumage and their intelligent nature made them popular as pets. They were also a favorite of street musicians who played a barrel organ while holding a trained parrot. Burrowing parrots were also threatened by habitat loss as much of the local area became dominated by cattle ranches.

When the reserve was set up, protection was put in place and a large cattle ranch was removed. Without thousands of grazing cattle, native plants have been regrowing, flowering and producing seeds that the burrowing parrots eat. Among their favorites are the silvery seedpods of French broom and the seeds of boldo trees.

Now that the parrots are protected and have plenty to eat, more chicks are being born and more are surviving. There used to be just three colonies, but as they grew bigger some parrots flew off and started new ones. Now there are 15 colonies inside the reserve and two outside. The hope is that the parrots will soon start moving back into other places where they used to live.

# Bringing Back the Quolls

Three hours' drive from the Australian city of Sydney, bordering the white beaches and sparkling waters of Jervis Bay, there's a thriving wild place. Booderee National Park is home to at least 200 bird species, from noisy friarbirds and beautiful firetails to little penguins and powerful owls. There are tawny frogmouths and snake-necked turtles, swamp wallabies and echidnas, and a curious native marsupial, covered in spots, with an inquisitive whiskery nose and a big appetite for spiders. For over 50 years, eastern quolls were extinct on the Australian mainland, but a few years ago they were brought back to Booderee.

Like many of Australia's native marsupial mammals, eastern quolls were wiped out by wild cats and foxes introduced by settlers. Fortunately, they survived on the island of Tasmania. The quolls that were brought back to Booderee weren't taken from the Tasmanian wild but carefully bred in captivity. Following several releases, quolls are now once again breeding in the wild on the Australian mainland.

The program has been a success because foxes are kept out of Booderee. The park is owned by the Wreck Bay Aboriginal Community who have cared for the land and waters of Jervis Bay for generations. They help to manage the park using a mix of traditional knowledge and modern science.

Bringing eastern quolls back is about more than restoring a missing species. They're helping restore balance to nature. Quolls play a key role in the animal food web, eating spiders and cockroaches, clearing up carrion, even hunting for non-native rabbits. Too many Australian species have been lost forever because nobody acted in time to save small populations from the brink. Quolls show that we must act now.

# Return of the Atlantic Bluefin Tuna

Atlantic bluefin tuna are the biggest of all the tuna. They can grow to the size of cars, with big, piercing eyes and warm blood flowing through their bodies. They also happen to be the most valuable fish in the Atlantic Ocean, which is why so many have been caught and for decades their numbers in the wild have been going down and down. But recently, things have been looking up and now Atlantic bluefins seem to be on the road to recovery.

The powerful muscles of bluefin tuna propel them on long migrations, or journeys, through the ocean and their fatty, red meat is highly prized for sushi, a traditional Japanese dish. For decades, bluefin tuna fisheries were not well controlled. Things got so bad that measures were introduced, based on advice from scientists, to reduce the number being caught. The Atlantic bluefin populations began regrowing and the species is no longer critically endangered.

Three other tuna species — yellowfin, albacore and southern bluefins — are also growing in number again thanks to checks on fishing. Not all tuna around in the world are doing so well. Bluefins in the Gulf of Mexico have not yet recovered from decades of overfishing and yellowfins in the Indian Ocean are still not being well looked after. In the Pacific, the population of another bluefin species remains tiny compared to what was there before commercial fishing began. However, the return of some tuna species shows that controlling fishing works. Catching fewer fish gives populations a chance to survive and grow.

# The Elephant Seals
# Staying Strong

It was not so long ago — just over a hundred years —
that people thought northern elephant seals had vanished forever.
These enormous, deep-diving marine mammals, with chunky
blubber and trunk-like snouts, were becoming a faded memory.

Hunters started killing elephant seals in California in the 1800s because whales
were getting harder to find and the world was still hungry for their oil. Seal blubber
was a good substitute. What's more, seals were much easier to catch than whales,
when they clambered onto beaches to molt and rear their pups. Hunters kept killing
elephant seals until none were left. In 1884, the species was declared extinct.

Then eight years later, eight of them showed up on the shore of Guadalupe Island,
off Mexico. Scientists decided to kill seven of them for museum collections. They
figured the species was already doomed so they may as well preserve what they could.
It was just a stroke of luck that those were not the last of the northern elephant seals.

Somewhere out of sight in the Pacific Ocean more seals held out. Scientists never
found them and hunters gave up looking. Slowly, the population recovered and seals
began returning to America's islands and beaches. Now northern elephant seals are
strictly protected and there's at least 150,000. Worries remain about their
future because they are at risk of disease and pollution, but the
northern elephant seals are no longer at high risk of extinction.
All they needed was for people to leave them be.

# Seabirds Steer Clear for Safety

The deep, cold sea off the coast of Namibia is full of plankton and fish. Industrial fishing boats work in these waters catching silvery fish like hake and mackerel. And for a long time, the fishing fleets also killed thousands of seabirds as they swooped and dived to grab the bait. Nobody wanted so many birds to die. To save them, the fishery needed to find a way to scare them off.

Around the world, seabirds get tangled in fishing nets, snagged on hooks and drowned. The Namibian hake fishery used to be one of the world's deadliest fisheries. The boats used to kill between 20,000 and 30,000 seabirds every year, including threatened species like the Atlantic yellow-nosed albatross and white-chinned petrels.

Like many industrial fisheries, these boats operate on a massive scale. They use longlines that stretch for miles and are covered in tens of thousands of baited hooks. It seemed like a huge task to stop seabirds trying to eat the bait, but in fact there was a simple answer. Brightly colored streamers fixed to the longlines are all it takes to scare most of the seabirds away. Adding weights also helps the lines sink quickly out of reach from the flapping birds.

After several years of hard work by Birdlife International's Albatross Task Force, the fishing boats in Namibia began using bird-scaring lines — and it has worked. The bird death rate has dropped by more than 98 percent. This saves at least 20,000 birds every year. The program is also helping female empowerment in Namibia. A local women's group, Meme Itumbapo, makes and sells the bird-scaring lines. The Albatross Task Force hopes similar projects will help save seabirds in other parts of the world in the future.

# The Kiwi Walk of Recovery

Every year in May, people across Te Tai Tokerau in Aotearoa (Northland, New Zealand) stay up late, walk out into the dark night and carefully listen. What they hope to hear is a high-pitched, whistling screech or a rasping squawk — the sounds of kiwi. Combined with recording devices that are set out every five years, Northlanders are hearing kiwi returning to patches of forest that used to be empty and silent.

There are five species of kiwi. All of them strut about on stout legs, their tiny wings invisible under a tufty wig of hair-like feathers. They have dark, beady eyes and poor eyesight, made up for by other senses including a strong sense of smell. They have a long beak with nostrils at the end to sniff out food. Kiwis are threatened by the destruction of their forest homes and by certain predators. Before people arrived, there were no native mammals on Aotearoa, except for a few species of harmless bat. But this changed as more and more people came to the islands, introducing predators including dogs, cats, rats and stoats. Dogs can't resist the smell of kiwi, so they chase after and catch them, and stoats eat kiwi chicks.

There used to be at least 12 million kiwis in Aotearoa, but fewer than 100,000 kiwi are left. Te Tai Tokerau is the only place where kiwi are doing well outside of areas with fencing to keep predators out or on remote islands. Local community groups are working in partnership to help kiwi, by trapping pest animals, like rodents and feral cats, and encouraging people to keep their dogs under control. Their efforts are paying off. At Whangārei Heads there used to be just 80 kiwi and now there are at least a thousand. Plus, work to help kiwi helps other native animals like fantail birds and pāteke ducks that also live in Aotearoa's forests.

# Releasing Giant Clams into the Wild

Giant clams look like crinkled smiles grinning up from the seabed with colorful lipstick in gleaming turquoise, greens and blues. These relatives of snails and scallops make the biggest shells in the world and can weigh as much as two baby elephants. On many coral reefs around the world, giant clams have become rare because people eat them and use their shells as decorations. 40 years ago, around the islands of the Philippines, giant clams almost disappeared, until a team of marine biologists stepped in.

When Edgardo Gomez from the University of the Philippines saw that giant clams were vanishing from his country, he asked marine biologists on nearby islands for help. In the Solomon Islands and Palau these huge, shelled creatures were doing better. People there collected baby giant clams, called larvae, that are tiny and swim around, and sent them to Edgardo. His team then kept the little clams in aquarium tanks until they grew to the size of a human hand. Then they put them in a nursery area, a place on the seabed where the young clams could grow up safely inside wire cages that made sure they didn't get eaten by nibbling fish. When the clams were big enough to survive on their own, Edgardo's team planted them out on coral reefs all across the Philippines, saving them from extinction.

People are still growing clams in the Philippines. There's a seabed nursery the size of seven soccer fields that holds around 30,000 enormous clams. Slowly people are learning to love giant clams and appreciate them when they're still alive. The university has launched an adopt-a-clam program to help raise money and educate people about these huge, gentle giants.

# Saving Slow-moving Snails

In the middle of the Pacific Ocean, on a group of tropical islands, there used to live dozens of species of little snails. Local people collected their empty spiralling shells to make into traditional crowns and necklaces for special celebrations. Scientists who were studying how the snails evolved into so many species realized they were vanishing. To save the slow-moving snails, they needed to act fast.

Polynesian tree snails, or Partula as scientists named them, were heading towards extinction in a snail-eats-snail story. Several decades ago, people brought in giant African land snails to the islands of Polynesia as a source of food. But soon those enormous snails escaped and began munching the local plant life. Rosy wolf snails were released to hunt the giant snails, but instead the rosy wolf snails started eating the Partula snails as well.

As soon as scientists understood why Partula snails were disappearing they collected as many species as they could find and sent them to zoos around the world. Some species were already extinct, but many were saved.

Captive breeding of Partula snails has been a great success. Organized by the Zoological Society of London, zookeepers shared knowledge and together worked out how to keep the snails in plastic containers. You can see Partula conservation in action in zoos across Europe and North America, including in London, Riga and Detroit. The plan wasn't just to breed snails for people to see – tens of thousands have been taken back to Polynesia and released into the wild.

There's a similar story on other Pacific islands, including Hawai'i, where rosy wolf snails were also released to control giant land snails. Some Hawaiian tree snails have gone extinct but some are being kept alive in captivity and released into secret spots in remote forests. Scientists hope Partula and other tree snails will return in great numbers and once again be at the heart of the islands' cultures and traditions.

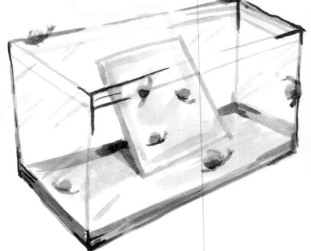

# Making Vultures Safe

Soaring high on windy thermals is where you would normally expect to see a vulture. But they have been vanishing faster than any other birds on the planet. Across India, Nepal, Pakistan and Bangladesh vultures were dropping dead, and nobody could work out why. Then a team of researchers from Pakistan and the Peregrine Fund discovered that vultures were being poisoned.

The vultures weren't deliberately being killed, but they were dying because farmers gave sick cows a medicine to treat pain and inflammation. When cows die, it's traditional in Asia to leave their bodies out for vultures to deal with. Vultures provide nature's free animal disposal service. A small flock can clear all the meat from the bones in just an hour. But if a cow was given the medicine a few days before it died, their meat is deadly for vultures. The birds suffer from kidney failure and die.

The numbers of white-rumped, red-headed, Indian and Egyptian vultures have dropped enormously. This has hit not just the species but whole ecosystems and people too. Instead of vultures cleaning up dead cattle, packs of scavenging wild dogs have moved in, causing the spread of rabies, a deadly disease that can be passed on by animal bites.

Scientists spotted the problem and the medicine has been banned in many countries. An alternative, non-toxic treatment for cows was identified and slowly, the vulture crisis is being turned around.

Scientists tag vultures, monitor their locations and count them while slowly driving along the same roads, and they have seen the birds coming back more and more. Vultures also seem to be doing better in the Thar Desert in Pakistan. Several Vulture Safe Zones have been set up where vultures are given untreated cattle to eat that are drug-free and allowed to die naturally of old age.

# Scimitar-horned Oryx Trotting Home

Magnificent long, curving horns belong to an antelope called the scimitar-horned oryx. For decades they were extinct in their wild habitats on the edge of the Sahara in Africa. They disappeared following long years of fighting and civil war when hunting was out of control. But herds of oryx were rescued and sent to zoos and ranches around the world. The hope was that when the situation calmed down, some of these oryx could be brought back to their homelands.

While the oryx were living in captivity, conservationists around the world worked together to make sure the animals did not suffer from inbreeding. This can happen when herds are too small and the adults are too closely related to each other, leading to health problems within the group. Captive oryx in different countries were sent to Abu Dhabi to set up a 'world herd' with plenty of diversity, which should help the animals survive back in the wild.

In 2017 and 2018, the scimitar-horned oryx were released in the central African country of Chad, where the species had used to roam. They live in a large nature reserve that has suitable habitat for oryx and they settled in quickly. The reserve is also home to lots of other endangered desert animals, including dorcas gazelles and dama gazelles, which means it is a hopeful place for oryx too. The animals were all given electronic collars so conservationists can track them and see how they are getting on. Not long after the oryx herds were reintroduced some of the females gave birth. These were the first scimitar-horned oryx calves born in the wild in 30 years.

## Our Wild Habitats
# Forests

Trees are amazing green giants. They tower into the sky and grab energy from the Sun to make food for themselves and for masses of animals that live in them — orangutans, gorillas, lemurs, toucans, squirrels, snakes, even kangaroos! Down underground, there's a web of roots and fungi that help trees talk to each other, share food and care for each other - like a family. This is known as the 'wood wide web' and it links all the trees across a forest.

There are several different types of forest. Tropical rainforests grow in steamy places near the equator, like the forests where tigers or Polynesian tree snails live. Trees also grow in cooler places, like the forests and woodlands where kiwi and checkered skipper butterflies live. Dry forests grow where it doesn't rain for much of the year, like the forests in Madagascar where chameleons live. Near the poles there are snow forests, also called boreal forests or taiga. They are home to animals like great grey owls, bears and lynx. Forests can be evergreen, which means the trees keep their leaves all year-round, or deciduous, where they drop their leaves in winter or during the dry season. Altogether, forests cover a third of the Earth's land area and they're incredibly important for biodiversity, which is the variety of life on Earth. Forests are home to eight out of ten of all the species on land.

Forests clean the air that we breathe and they are crucial
in the fight against climate change. Trees soak up loads of
carbon from the atmosphere and store it in their trunks and soil.
When trees are cut down or burned, the carbon is released as the
gas carbon dioxide, making climate change worse by trapping heat
in the atmosphere. Trees also provide jobs, food and materials,
especially for indigenous people who have special ties
to the places where they live.

Sadly, forests are being damaged and destroyed, often through
the process of deforestation (cutting down trees). More forests are
burning, possibly because climate change is drying them out.
This threatens not just the trees themselves but also the animals
that live there, so it's important that we act now to save our forests.

The good news is that when we leave forests alone, they can
grow back. Forests are naturally regrowing in Canada, central
Africa, Mongolia and Brazil. These recovering forests have grown
over a total area the same size as France. With new forest
conservation projects and nature reserves protecting trees from
being cut down, there is hope for the forests of our planet,
but there is always more work to be done!

# Oceans

Earth is very blue. Around three-quarters of our planet is covered with water. Different parts have been given names: the Indian, Pacific, Atlantic, Arctic and Southern Oceans, as well as smaller areas like the Caribbean Sea and the North Sea.

Ocean life comes in many shapes and sizes. There are enormous blue whales and the tiny animals they eat, called plankton. There are spiny sea urchins and boneless jellyfish, rainbow-colored butterflyfish and inky black dragonfish. Some marine animals stay mostly in one place, like seahorses. Others go on great long journeys, like sea turtles.

There are lots of important habitats in the ocean. A quarter of all the ocean's species are found on coral reefs. Corals themselves are tiny animals, related to sea anemones and jellyfish, which build solid structures that help protect land from storms and waves. Mangrove forests are made of trees that survive with their roots and trunks growing in salty water. Baby fish hide among the flooded roots and when they are older move out to the open sea. Mangroves store lots of carbon and are important for reducing climate change, as are seagrass meadows. In cold seas, there are underwater forests made of giant seaweed called kelp. These provide shelter and food for sea otters, octopuses, sharks, sunflower sea stars and many more species.

The deep ocean, anything below 650 feet, is the part we know least about. People used to think it was so dark and cold nothing lived down there. But now we know the deep ocean is full of life. Scientists are always discovering amazing deep-sea species, like yeti crabs with long furry arms and worms with scales like glittering sequins. Important habitats in the deep include scorching hot springs called black smokers and giant underwater volcanoes called seamounts.

People also used to think the ocean was too big to harm. Sadly that's not true. Plastic garbage flows along rivers and out to sea. When aquanauts visited the ocean's deepest point, the Mariana Trench in the western Pacific Ocean, they found plastic bags and candy wrappers. Too much fishing in the ocean means many species are now rare, including bluefin tuna and hammerhead sharks. Climate change is causing heat waves in the ocean which wipe out coral reefs and kelp forests. It's also getting much noisier in the ocean, mainly from shipping, and animals like whales have trouble hearing each other.

Although the ocean has many problems, there's still room for hope. One way to help the ocean is to set up marine reserves, like Cabo Pulmo. More reserves like this will help us protect all of our ocean habitats and the creatures that call them home.

Our Wild Habitats

# Polar Regions

Far to the north and south are the coldest, iciest places on Earth —
the Arctic and Antarctic. On the snowy land and in the frozen seas
there are species that can survive in these extreme conditions.

In the Arctic, polar bears roam the ice that covers the sea, hunting
seals when they come up to breathe. Polar bears also hunt for
narwhals, whales with long, twisting tusks. It's a mystery how narwhals
use their tusks, but maybe they hunt, sense or fight with them.
Bowhead whales keep warm in the Arctic with a very thick layer of
fat under their skin, called blubber. Sometimes they even get too
hot and swim around with their mouths open to cool down.

Many animals hide from each other in the snowy land of
the Arctic, which is known as tundra - another word for a
cold, flat place with no trees. Arctic foxes and snowy owls
sneak up on prey, including white Arctic hares.

Down south, in Antarctica, live a different set of
animals. There are many penguin species, including
chinstrap, gentoo and Adélies. Emperor penguins
are the biggest at more than three feet tall. Through
the dark, frozen Antarctic winters, emperor
penguins huddle together on
the ice, raising their chicks.

Antarctica is a huge continent that's covered in ice and surrounded by the coldest ocean on Earth, the Southern Ocean. Important animals in the Southern Ocean are krill, which are relatives of crabs and lobsters. Huge shoals of krill can be seen from space. Krill are the main food for whales, seals, fish and seabirds. People catch krill too, using huge ships and enormous nets. Then they crush them into food for pets and farmed fish, like salmon.

The North and South poles are a long way apart but there are some species that live around both, like orca and Arctic terns. Each year, Arctic terns fly from the Arctic to Antarctica. Throughout their lives, Arctic terns fly a distance equivalent to that of going to the moon and back three times!

Climate change is the biggest threat to the frozen poles. Parts of the Arctic and Antarctic are warming much faster than anywhere else. Frozen soil in the Arctic, called permafrost, is melting and releasing methane, which is a greenhouse gas like carbon dioxide, making climate change worse. Melting ice also contributes towards rising sea levels, which will impact many people living on coasts and islands around the world. Snow and ice reflect the Sun's heat and help cool the planet so it's important that we protect these special habitats. Conservationists around the world are learning about and fighting climate change, aiming to give these icy polar regions, and the amazing animals who live there, the best chances for the future.

# Our Wild Habitats
# Wetlands

Freshwater trickles, pours, flows and soaks into the places in nature known as wetlands, and they are full of amazing wildlife. Rivers, lakes, streams, ponds, salt marshes and peat bogs together cover about six percent of the Earth's surface but are home to at least a 100,000 species.

The Amazon River is the world's biggest river by volume. It's home to manatees, giant otters, river dolphins, and spotty stingrays. Red-bellied piranhas also live in the river and talk by barking and croaking. In Africa, Lake Victoria, Lake Tanganyika and Lake Malawi are home to thousands of colorful fish called cichlids. Some cichlids lay eggs in empty shells and some look after their babies inside their mouths.

In total, more than half of the world's fish species live in wetlands, the rest live in the sea, and some go on great journeys between the two. Eels are born at sea then swim thousands of miles towards land and up rivers where they stay and grow. Many years later, when they are ready to find a mate, eels swim back out to sea.

Wetlands are linked to the sea by water that's always on the move, in what we call the water cycle. When the Sun heats the sea, freshwater evaporates into the air, leaving salt behind. This freshwater becomes clouds and eventually falls as rain which fills up all the world's wetlands. Water flows along streams and rivers and eventually back out to sea.

Wetlands do many important things. Salt marshes grow at the edges of the sea and help protect coasts from storms. Peat bogs store twice as much carbon as all the world's forests put together. But the world's wetlands are in danger. They are disappearing three times faster than forests. Farmers drain wetlands and plant crops in their place. Rivers and lakes are polluted with plastics and chemicals from farmland and industrial waste. Peat bogs are dug up to sell as garden compost. When this happens, carbon that was stored underground is turned into carbon dioxide gas which adds to the problem of climate change.

The good news is that around the world people are starting to look after wetlands. In Indonesia, where channels used to be cut to drain peat bogs, people are now blocking those channels so the bogs fill back up with water. In England, people created new salt marshes by taking down sea walls and letting the tide flood in.

Species are also returning to wetlands. Giant Amazonian fish, called arapaima, were being overfished and are now doing much better because local people are protecting them. In Great Britain, the River Thames is much cleaner than it once was and many animals, like seals and seahorses, are living there again. Keeping up work like this means a safer future for Earth's wetlands and their many inhabitants.

# Deserts, Grasslands and Savannas

There are deserts all around the world, from the Thar Desert in India where vultures are returning, to the Sahara where scimitar-horned oryx now roam again. Together, deserts cover a fifth of all the land area.

Deserts can be scorching hot and freezing cold — sometimes both in the same day. In Asia's Gobi Desert it can be 104 degrees farenheit during the summer and minus 68 degrees farenheit in winter. It might not rain for months in the desert, so it is always very dry, but plants and animals have amazing ways of living in deserts without drying out, boiling or turning into blocks of ice.

Fennec foxes from the Sahara have huge ears. Their ears lose heat, and help cool their bodies. Thick fur protects them on hot sand and keeps them warm at night. Like many desert animals, fennec foxes spend their days in cool burrows underground then come out at night to eat. They don't drink but get all the water they need from their food.

Unexpected animals can also be found living in deserts, including fish and frogs. Devil's Hole pupfish live in an underground lake in a cave in Death Valley in America. Desert spadefoot frogs live in the deserts of Western Australia and spend months underground, covered in a cocoon made of dead skin that stops them drying out.

Cactuses survive in deserts by soaking up and storing water in their huge trunks. In the mountain-top deserts of Hawaii, Āhinahina plants are covered in silvery hairs which reflect the sun and keep them cool. Lots of plant seeds lie in the ground and when it finally rains they grow very quickly. When flowers bloom, birds like the jewel-colored Costa's hummingbirds swoop in to feed on sweet liquid called nectar. Desert plants also create homes for animals like elf owls that live in holes made in cactuses by woodpeckers.

Grasslands and savannas are mixtures of grass and woodlands that grow in places where it rains more. These are home to all sorts of animals. The Serengeti in Tanzania is full of elephants, cheetahs, lions, zebras and huge herds of wildebeest, a type of antelope. Other grasslands include prairies of North America and pampas of South America.

Deserts, grasslands and savannas are all at risk from climate change. Even though the animals and plants living there are tough, they may not survive if their homes get hotter. Climate change brings more wildfires that destroy these fragile habitats. Although some animals are losing their desert homes, many are thriving as people work to protect them and their natural habitats. These success stories show how nature can bounce back when given a helping hand.

# Meet the Nature Champions

**Jeremy Thomas** is a British insect detective (otherwise known as an entomologist) who has devoted his career to saving insect species. He laid trails of cake crumbs to find red ant nests and worked out they are vital for large blue butterflies.

Koori people of the **Wreck Bay Aboriginal Community** are the traditional owners of **Booderee National Park**. Families pass on special knowledge about the animals and plants, and how to find food and medicines in nature.

The **Arhuaco people** of the Sogrome community live in Sierra Nevada de Santa Marta in Colombia. Starry night harlequin toads, which they call gouna, are sacred to the community and they are supporting scientists in their work to protect them.

A team of scientists from Madagascar and Germany rediscovered Voeltzkow's chameleon in 2018. They were part of the **Rewild project** which works to find, protect and restore rare and lost species around the world.

The **Meme Itumbapo Women's Group** in Namibia make devices that scare off seabirds and stop them getting killed by fishing boats. **Samantha Matjila** from the **Namibia Nature Foundation** goes to sea and shows fishermen how to use them.

**Sylvia Earle** leads Mission Blue, an organization which picked **Cabo Pulmo National Marine Park** in Mexico as one of 140 'Hope Spots' (special places that are vital for a healthy ocean). Local people are at the heart of the park, exploring the reef and learning about the animals on their doorstep.

**Susannah Calderan** from the Scottish Association for Marine Science and **Jennifer Jackson** from the British Antarctic Survey led the study of blue whales in South Georgia. They have studied the sounds whales and dolphins make and how the creatures are recovering.

**The Kiwi Coast** is group of thousands of people working together to help the kiwi of Te Tai Tokerau, Aotearoa. Every year, they run the Kiwi Call Count Survey, where people listen for kiwis and report the results with a smartphone app.

**Fatou Janha** from The Gambia set up the **TRY Oyster Women's Association** to support the community who gather oysters and cockles from a mangrove forest. The women protect the forest and earn money to support their families.

**Paolo Fanciulli** is a fisherman from Italy. When big trawling boats fished illegally and destroyed seagrass meadows he asked artists to sculpt one hundred marble blocks. He put them in the sea to keep the boats away.

**Jacqueline Evans** led a five-year campaign to set up **Marae Moana**, a plan that looks after the whole ocean area of the Cook Islands. The plan includes reserves which protect the rich biodiversity across almost 8 million square miles of ocean.

**Gab Mejia**, from the Philippines, is a young writer and photographer who set up **Youth Engaged in Wetlands**, which brings together young people in 30 countries to protect wetlands around the world.

When he was 12, **Lesein Mutunkei**, from Kenya, decided to plant a tree every time he scored a goal in soccer. He has planted more than a thousand trees and set up **Trees for Goals**, a project that educates young people about climate change and deforestation.

**Bayarjargal Agvaantseren** from Mongolia helped to create a huge nature reserve in the South Gobi Desert to protect snow leopards. She persuaded the government to stop plans for 37 mines inside the reserve.

**Lisa Carne** set up **Fragments of Hope** in Belize. Divers take small fragments of coral from healthy reefs and move them to damaged areas, where they grow bigger and help reefs to recover.

**Thai Van Nguyen** founded **Save Vietnam's Wildlife**. He has saved thousands of pangolins from the illegal wildlife trade and set up a center to care for rescued pangolins. These scaly mammals are endangered because people think their scales cure all sorts of illnesses.

In villages in Assam, India, **Purnima Devi Barman** set up the **Hargila Army**, a group of women who protect hargila — one of the world's rarest storks. Purnima helped local people to learn to love the storks as their own special species.

On Timor Island in Indonesia, **Aleta Baun** led hundreds of Mollo women in a peaceful protest to protect sacred forests from mining companies. For a year, they sat on the land and weaved traditional cloth until eventually the mining companies gave up.

Marine biologist **Ali Badreddine** changed how fishermen in Lebanon think about sea turtles. In the past when turtles got caught in their nets, fishermen would kill them. Thanks to Ali, they now set them free.

**Nemonte Nenquimo** is a Waorani woman from Ecuador who won a legal battle to protect her home in the Amazon rainforest from being drilled for oil. She inspires many other indigenous people to stand up and say no to the destruction of their homelands.

**Edgardo Gomez** set up the **Marine Science Institute** in the Philippines and was a pioneer in growing endangered giant clams to release into the wild. He helped save several species from going extinct.

# Conclusion
# The Wild Will Go On

Nature is precious and important in so many ways and, even when times are hard, it can be tough and bounce back from trouble. Through the stories in this book, we've seen snails and insects, birds and mammals, plants, reptiles and fish that are all doing much better with the help of passionate people taking strong action.

So much more of the wild world needs help to survive and thrive, and there's lots of work still to do. But now we know what actions work. Sometimes it's a matter of stopping the hunting and killing of so many animals, which isn't always as easy as it sounds. Sometimes there are problems that need clever ways to solve them. Often, by protecting wild places many species can be saved too.

There isn't one perfect way to save all of nature, but lots of different actions need to be taken. Together we can push in the right direction and make a real change.

The wild world is going to keep on changing and it will need new ideas and more people to care about nature and help protect it in any way possible. Maybe one of those people could be you!

# Wherever you live, you can make a difference and help the wild world. Here are some ideas:

- Only put things in the toilet or sink that naturally break down (toilets and sinks connect to rivers and eventually to the sea), so no plastics or nasty chemicals.

- Use dishwashing liquid and laundry soap with fewer damaging chemicals (look for eco-friendly labels) and set your washing machine at lower temperatures to save energy.

- Eat less meat and more plants, and eat sustainable seafood which has been caught without harming the environment.

- Use fewer things made of single-use plastics, like throwaway plastic bottles.

- If you visit the seaside, join a beach clean-up or litter picker.

- If you go swimming in the sea, use eco-friendly sunscreen.

- If you have a garden, go peat-free and use alternative types of compost, make your own wetland by digging a wildlife pond, and plant more trees!

- Buy things made from recycled paper and don't buy toothpaste, food and other things containing palm oil, which often comes from places where forests were cut down.

- Talk about the wild world to other people. Help spread the word that nature is in trouble, but all is not lost and there's still plenty we can do to help.

For August and Anouk.
H.S.

Dedicated to all those people working to make a brighter future
for our planet, and our little wildlings Bia, Tove, Ernie and Kit.
G.W.&W.